# NOT FOR AMNESIA

## Lo Galluccio

Červená Barva Press
Somerville, Massachusetts

Červená Barva Press
P.O. Box 440357
W. Somerville, MA 02144-3222

www.cervenabarvapress.com
Bookstore: www.thelostbookshelf.com

Cover art: "Night view of Brooklyn Bridge" (1982) Wikimedia

Cover Design: William J. Kelle
Production: Steve Asmussen

ISBN: 978-1-950063-81-9

# CONTENTS

# NOT FOR AMNESIA

*Dedicated to Stevie Smith whose child-like rhymes once inspired me to pen my own.*

*For Adam.*

# Not for Amnesia

# Adam

Your memory flew
up the tongue
of spring
pink and feathered
like silk.
So cruel
in my crotch
I save the grin shins,
sit birds chirping
my back.
Shivering I admire
asparagus bones
picketing a spot
on the table.
As aphids veil skin,
a blue bulb
chalks my brain,
and I crave
blankness.
The uterus drips
speed into my cup,
no howling kiss
from your mouth.
A cat bleeding air,
my desire
comes before
the world wars.
The decline of
our empire is the knot
in my stare.

# On Bugs

The outpour of impressions,
he can't stand that,

a calliope of other people's words
I blow,

shuts him like venetian blinds
in the sun.

Snatches I repeat
a machine on record, then play.
Too solid to absorb miscellany,
he hates bugs

defying his shield of concentration,
zeroing in to prick him.

They don't rattle me.
a jungle inside, I may

Switch into a snake
disdaining desserts

and swallow the rats whole.

# A Fly

A fly
frying in the sky,
nothing acceptable to eat,

of hunger from
a stomach full of defeat.

Too vain in hunger
for anything like meat.

(A notion of nothing
replies to silence

in the sigh of why:
Not to shoot skeet.)

"A poem for the middle of the week."

    1.   A fly in the why.
    2.   A veil over my feet.
    3.   A belly grumbling in the heat of a leak.

A leak dribs to the ground.

A leak for the frying
and sighing of a sound.

A tweak for the meat
of defeat. In the middle
of a still hungry week.

The fly is ravenous: meek.

# Burial Ground

Because she may break he waits,
and the trees stiffen in all directions.

Folded against the building
like something collapsible, her long hair
a black stream.

He looks down on her curse
as limbs drying
the sky.

The trees
planted singly
not herded onto reservations.

She's the Navajo, the girl.
Will she remain cradling her bones
against the cement?

What of rain falling from her face,
the fish that may leap from her hair?

# Boo Hoo

Every red see-through door slammed
without a peek-a-boo game.

Repeatedly they slammed
my lungs until my heart
came and the juice fell
through my eyes of an exploding apple.

No, you said, no slamming
you said. It wouldn't shut.
The problem is it won't shut.

My breasts felt strange,
more foreign, less like fruit.
Marmoreal's the word
I couldn't remember.

Wind shoving tree hands
against my window like a schoolyard
brat as the bulldog and lamb
lay gravely inanimate.

Faceless gods
with long-fingered hands,
all long-fingered hands laughed
up a storm and I trembled:

Boo hoo, where are you?
Boo hoo, without you what'll I do?

# CANYON

The slick stuff in the pink jar,
a white cat glittering eyes green;
the black and tan bruises
of your hands on my mind.

The lonely rub of a lover married.
The ice blue of a dead one smoking,
a spire of light that seethes
in spite of the seagull choking.

Black clam stranded on the sand,
the burrowing germ of our lost plan,
fire in the eyes of a hungry god.
The digging your mouth couldn't take.

The dream I can't quite forsake.
A green turns yellow.
Red of the bake.
The punch of the drunk when he sees,

spilling laughter in trees.
Orange of mating, yellow of pain.
The tangles of chatter,
feet and heart freeze.

The desert, the cactus disease,
mourning of pink, silence of white,
The melody of hope sinking tight,
killing fever, damage done,

Echo, the echo, the loss
of someone.

# Santa Fe

Is this really what you want
she thought and asked
she thought and asked
and basked in the absence
of an answer.

You're a drop, he said,
like a drop in bed
like a drop in bed
that soaks up the dread,
You're a deep one, a deep one,
a deep.

When you smile
she winked,
When you smile
she winked,
You take me to Paris,
You take me away
to a place I could stay,
Paris, a moment,
a day.

As my lover, he said,
As my lover, he said,
with his hands
with his pulse
as my lover you'll find
the salt and the pounce.

I want them she thought.
I want them she said.

Do this, do this:
Don't stop. Don't stop
till our blood
is bluer than anger.
Redder than.  The price
Of this fever is, fever is.

# THE PIPER

You whine for sleep your mouth
sawing itself and curse
what splinters your head,

a forgotten language.
Ache for baptism.

Dread the game of day.
Sniffing its corridor for clear water

and salvation.  Anything to defeat
vibrations of civilization

you come to lost.  Ready to squeeze
his morning juice from traces

at your throat.  In his gaze
fire fades to smoke
sacking your lungs

like a botched theatrical effect.
A cold so thorough it rains
slugs your senses, no parasol of memory
to smatter its fists.

# The Sphinx

You're wrapped and gathered, writing.
            A lipsticked smile.
Legs under you pelican-like
        the smell of your bosom again.


        Your grandfather a God and clock
we ration our voices to.  Ticking up
            my Lore
        in mahogany shine.


        After flat chants,
dim sum phrases,
    I go home a waiter ,
        from a bad shift, grotesque,
no good tips.

# THE OFFICE POEM

For a circular someone,
linear's a drilling lame,
the same same.
Until variety's cred out
sped to doubt.  Notoriety can't shout.
Smaller, slacker, with bead-oil eyes.
Corrupt and clean in your veins.

# THE STREET'S SWEET

Unisex replete.

The real Santa dipped it
in hot wax and electrified.

Santa froze at

male dogs with thick bones,
female cats have thin smiles.

The street's sweet
unisex replete.

# Solitaire A.

I wonder now at all
my lost strength
and the illusion of it.
How I grew phony eyes
of green and never paused
to know it.

I wonder with these
skies so hot and grey
and still.  I wonder
how I lost them
for the beauty of one pill.

For love and all
its vastness, for love
and all its pain.  I wonder
will I love and couple
with a man, a bird, a brain?

Will I love again?

# QUARANTINE

Blue feet,
scales up the back
hot dimes in shoulder blades…
A name for love like
ammonia, January, fear.

When I awake, union's far removed.
In one butterfly wing I dreamt:

the space of your nose distant,
a taste in your mouth filament.

Some toothless god smiling,
a goddess twines

your Chelsea cave.  No matter
how long deep or wet, our souls
are shy of meshing,
and we're the meshing kind.

Steep white like Andes.
Cattle bone of moans.
A sea black rattling.
Crackling roses
are popcorn poses engraved.

We are saved.
We are saved.

# Self-Pity with Lipstick

I was a girl
who ran at the fudge,
dove for the race-lines
ground through some glory,
now can't budge.

A girl
A sick angel behind her
spurred her, stirred her,
bound and tied her
to a long death glider.

A girl
with a rage and a sting,
took sick in the ring,
lost her place on the page
in search of a sage
fanning fling.

Bad Brooklyn in my face.
Hungering for enchantment,
a boiling brook to cook
the brew of my encampment.

"Amnesia" whisper voices,
for deliverance and form,
cleave to form,
your nipples kit there.

Let content slip,
slip bare.  Let it drip
through the silver sieve,

truth slither, a dither
a doo.  Jiggle pieces,
slash beef, make do.

Suck the whip, girl, you.

# INSECT DANCE

Settle then for smallness, infinitesimal vantage
of ants, push your picnic crumbs to safer zones.
Steal away to huts knick-knacked with baubles
to kittle and portend.  Wee those charms,
      souvenirs. Spun
haunts strewn with polaroids, structured
salads and survivors.  Tourists to the tundra
warm slowly, gain edge from
      glass.  Industry
      an ice-mold cutting teeth against
      Eternity. Like
a dirigible leaks, dangles humans from helium.
Hover earth's waters, erode imaginatively
through holiday spats.  To light,
blow out.  Lucky lips to matches.
Our spooky, sacred hatches.

# Acknowledgments

The poem "Adam" first appeared in the chapbook *Terrible Baubles*, 2009.

# Special Thanks

To my ex roommate Karen Lucky, my friend Jane Bordal, my ex-boy-friend, Adam Gorgoni, the late Eddie Sperry, Richard Cambridge, my dear friend, Marc Zegans who encouraged me to publish this early work, my mother, brother and sister, and to Gloria Mindock of Červená Barva Press for publishing it.

# About the Author

Lo's first published release is *Hot Rain*, a poetry collection on Ibbetson Street Press, followed by *Sarasota VII* a prose poem memoir on Červená Barva Press. In 2010, Alternating Current Press released *Terrible Baubles* which was also made into spoken word CD with music. She's been nominated for four Pushcart Prizes in poetry. Her other two CDs as a vocalist are *Being Visited* on the Knitting Factory label and *Spell on You*, a self-release. They can be heard on Bandcamp, Spotify and Amazon Prime. Lo served as Poet Populist of Cambridge between 2013-2015. She completed her MFA in creative writing from Stonecoast in July 2019. Her work has appeared in *Litkicks.com, www.strangeroad.com, The Heat City Literary Review, The Solstice Literary Review, Night magazine, Home Anthology, Eden Waters Press, Lungfull magazine!, Constellations Journal, Wilderness House Literary Review, Ibbetson Street, The Oddball Review, Muddy River Review*, among others. She's performed at the Boston Poetry Festival and the New York City New Year's Day Poetry Marathon for the Poetry Project. She currently lives in Cambridge, MA with her cat Lucy, an aloof tabby, but has drawn most of her inspiration from New York City where she lived between 1991 and 2001 on the Lower East Side.